****

IMPOSTERS AMONG US

****

➤➤➤ By Virginia Loh-Hagan ◄◄◄

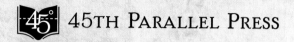

45TH PARALLEL PRESS

Published in the United States of America by Cherry Lake Publishing Group
Ann Arbor, Michigan
www.cherrylakepublishing.com

Reading Adviser: Beth Walker Gambro, MS, Ed., Reading Consultant, Yorkville, IL
Book Designer: Melinda Millward

Library of Congress Cataloging-in-Publication Data has been filed and is available at catalog.loc.gov.

Cherry Lake Publishing Group would like to acknowledge the work of the Partnership for 21st Century Learning, a Network of Battelle for Kids. Please visit http://www.battelleforkids.org/networks/p21 for more information.

Printed in the United States of America
Corporate Graphics

About the Author

Dr. Virginia Loh-Hagan is an author and educator. She is currently the Director of the Asian Pacific Islander Desi American (APIDA) Center at San Diego State University and the Co-Executive Director of The Asian American Education Project. She lives in San Diego with her very tall husband and very naughty dogs. To learn more about her, follow her on Instagram @vlohhagan.

Note from publisher: Websites change regularly, and their future contents are outside of our control. Supervise children when conducting any recommended online searches for extended learning opportunities.

✳✳✳✳✳✳✳✳✳✳✳✳
TABLE OF CONTENTS
✳✳✳✳✳✳✳✳✳✳✳✳

INTRODUCTION

* * * * * * * * * * *

Imagine pretending to be someone else. This is what **imposters** do. They trick people. They fool people. They tell many lies. They lie about their names. They lie about who they are.

Imposters need to keep their stories straight. They may make fake papers. They act with a lot of **confidence**. Confidence is feeling sure of oneself.

Imposters have many reasons for faking. Some want fame. Some want fortune. Some want a new life. Being someone else is better for them.

Lying all the time is hard. Imposters get caught. They miss details. They mix up their lies. It was easier to be someone else in the past. There were no photo ID cards. There was no internet. There was no **DNA testing**. These tests use genes to identify relatives. But people keep trying. Learn about famous imposters in history.

CURRENT CASE:

Scotland's Most Famous Imposter

* * * * * * * * * *

Brian MacKinnon was born in 1963. He wanted to be a doctor. He graduated from Bearsden Academy. It is a private school in Scotland. Then he went to a university. But he flunked out. He wanted to start over. At 32, he went back to Bearsden Academy. He pretended to be 17. He lost weight. He plucked out his facial hair. He called himself Brandon Lee. He said he was from Canada. He said his mother was an opera singer. He said she died in a car crash. He said his father was a professor who also died. He said he lived with his sick grandmother. People believed his story. At first, MacKinnon was nervous. He thought teachers would remember him. He stayed out of trouble. Since he could drive, he became popular. He made friends. He starred in a school play. He got good grades. He got into a university. He was finally able to study medicine. Then he got caught. Someone called the newspapers. He was exposed.

* * * * * * * * * * * *
FALSE MARGARET
(1260–1301)
* * * * * * * * * * * *

Margaret (1283–1290) was the "Maid of Norway." She was the only daughter of King Eric of Norway (1268–1299). Her mother was the daughter of King Alexander III (1241–1286). Alexander III was the king of Scotland. When he died, Margaret became the queen of Scotland. But she died on her way to Scotland.

A German woman saw an opportunity. She took a ship to Norway. She claimed to be Margaret. She said she was kidnapped and sold. But her lie didn't work. She became known as False Margaret. The real Margaret was young. False Margaret was 20 years older.

False Margaret was accused of **treason**. Treason is the crime of betraying one's country. She was burned at the stake.

Norwegians are known for their Viking ancestry. Ships like this one were common for the Vikings.

LAMBERT SIMNEL

(1477–1534)

In 1483, King Richard III (1452–1485) became king of England. He jailed his 2 nephews. He put them in the Tower of London. His nephews threatened his crown. They became the "Princes in the Tower." The princes later disappeared.

Four years later, King Richard III died. He died in battle. Henry VII (1457–1509) became king. Then Lambert Simnel appeared. He claimed to be one of the princes. This made him the rightful king.

A priest supported Simnel. He said Simnel escaped from the tower. Many people opposed Henry VII. They crowned Simnel king. They raised an army. They invaded England. Henry VII defeated them. He **pardoned** Simnel. Pardon means to forgive. Simnel became a servant in Henry VII's castle.

King Richard III imprisoned his 2 nephews in the Tower of London.

* * * * * * * * * * *
GEORGE PSALMANAZAR
(c. 1679–1763)
* * * * * * * * * * *

George Psalmanazar said he was from Taiwan. Taiwan is in Asia. He said a priest kidnapped him. He said the priest brought him to England. He had blond hair. He had blue eyes. He had a French accent.

In 1704, Psalmanazar wrote a book. He included drawings. He made up stories about Taiwan. He said priests there **sacrificed** children. Sacrifice means to kill someone as an offering to a god.

The Idol of the DEVIL

George Psalmanazar's stories are still available to read today.

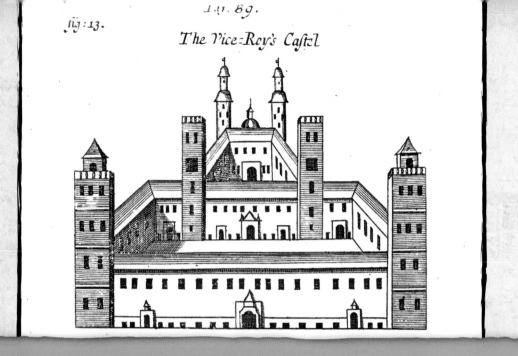

fig:13.

The Vice-Roy's Castle

George Psalmanazar had many illustrations included in his stories.

English people believed him. He became famous. (He was like a reality TV star.) But English **intellectuals** questioned him. Intellectuals are highly educated people. Psalmanazar gave nonsense answers. He was asked about his white skin. He said rich people in Taiwan lived underground.

He wrote a **confession**. Confessions are statements of truth. It was published after he died.

COLD CASE:

The Unsolved Mystery of the Fake Moscow Philharmonic

An orchestra is a big group of musicians. The Moscow Philharmonic (MPH) is an orchestra. It's in Russia. It's famous. It's respected. In 2000, someone called a stage manager in Hong Kong. The caller said MPH could play there. The Hong Kong government was excited. They agreed. The fake MPH played in August. They played a couple of shows. They played for more than 10,000 people. They made more than $30,000. They did a great job. They got good reviews. But they got caught. The real MPH was touring Europe. They were shocked. They couldn't be in 2 places at once. Hong Kong music-lovers were fooled. They felt shame. Some wanted their money back. But many enjoyed the show. It's still a mystery today. No one knows who the fake MPH members were. It's believed they were Russian musicians. Some may have been rejected from the real MPH.

* * * * * * * * * * * *

JOICE HETH
(c. 1756–1836)

* * * * * * * * * * * *

Joice Heth was an enslaved African American woman. P.T. Barnum (1810–1891) hosted a circus. Barnum used Heth as his first act. He said she was 161 years old. He said she was President George Washington's (1732–1799) nanny. Heth told stories about "little George."

Heth was blind. She could barely move. She didn't have teeth. Barnum was accused of pulling her teeth. He wanted to make her look older.

People questioned her age. When she died, Barnum let

a doctor examine her body. More than 1,500 people paid to watch. The doctor said the body was about 80 years old. Barnum said he used another body. He said Heth was alive. He said she was touring in Europe. Later, Barnum admitted the truth. People disapproved of how he **exploited** Heth. Exploit means to use for personal gain.

P.T. Barnum was the real imposter. He tricked people. He created many fake acts. Some people spoke out against Barnum.

He Has the Nerve to Say That
BARNUM WAS WRONG!

P.T. Barnum

Castle Garden in 1850

Barnum's Bridgeport home

One of Kodets Freaks

Lame John Kodet

Barnum Cunning

* * * * * * * * * * * *
MARGARET ANN BULKLEY
(1789–1865)
* * * * * * * * * * * *

Margaret Ann Bulkley was born in Ireland. She wanted to be a doctor. She wasn't allowed to go to school. She moved to London with her mother. Her mother's brother was James Barry. Barry died in 1806. Bulkley took his name. She became Dr. James Barry. She always wore a long coat. She wore high shoes to be taller. She finished medical school. She joined the British Army.

Bulkley was a great doctor. People thought she was too young. But they didn't think she was a woman. Women were supposed to be quiet. They were supposed to be gentle. Bulkley was not quiet. She got mad easily. She threw things. She got into fights.

When she died, Bulkley wanted to be buried in her clothes. She didn't want her body washed. Her wishes weren't followed. A nurse discovered her secret.

The British Army didn't require officers to get medical exams. That's how Margaret Ann Bulkley kept her secret.

MARY BAKER
(1792–1864)

In 1817, a young woman showed up in an English town. She wore foreign clothes. She looked lost. She spoke a strange language. She called herself "Caraboo."

A Portuguese sailor came to town. He talked to Caraboo. He said she was a princess from Indonesia. He said pirates kidnapped her. He said she jumped into the sea. That's how she landed in England.

Pretending to be a foreigner gave Mary Baker more sympathy.

Mary Baker became famous as Princess Caraboo. People raised money for her when they found out she was actually a beggar.

She became a hit. Newspapers wrote about her. Someone recognized her. She was a beggar. Her name was Mary Baker. Baker became a hero. She was a poor girl who tricked rich people. People liked that. They raised money for her. She moved to the United States. She still pretended to be Princess Caraboo. Later, Baker moved back to England. She married and had a daughter.

WORST-CASE SCENARIO:

Fake Survivors

* * * * * * * * * *

There have been awful events in history. Many people died. Many people suffered. Some people faked being there. They pretended to be survivors. Survivors are people who live through bad events. One horrible event was the Holocaust. This took place during World War II (1939–1945). The German Nazi Party killed many Jewish people in Europe. Some people pretended to be Holocaust survivors. Rosemarie Pence was one. She is a German American. She said she was Jewish. She said her name was Hannah. She said she was in a Nazi death camp. A book was written about her. She was caught in 2009.

Another awful event was the 9/11 attacks. Alicia Head was born in Spain in 1973. She said her name was Tania. She said she was at the World Trade Center when it was attacked. She joined a survivor support group. She became its leader. She was caught in 2007. She was in Spain when the towers fell.

SARAH EDMONDS

(1841–1898)

Sarah Edmonds worked on her family's farm. She wore men's farm clothes. Her father wanted her to marry. Instead, she ran away. Women didn't have much freedom. So she dressed like a man. She sold Bibles. She called herself Franklin Flint Thompson.

The Civil War (1861–1865) broke out. Edmonds joined. She served with the Union. She was in several battles. She was a male field nurse. She also claimed to be a spy. She acted like a man pretending to be a woman. Her spy name was Bridget O'Shea. She played other roles.

Edmonds got sick. She knew a military doctor would learn her secret. So she **deserted**. Deserting means to leave without permission. She worked as a nurse. She used her real name.

Sarah Edmonds dressed like a man and went by Franklin Flint Thompson. Edmonds wanted to fight for the Union Army in the Civil War.

BOU HMARA
(1860–1909)

Morocco is in northwest Africa. Bou Hmara served the **sultan**'s brother. A sultan is a king. Hmara got into trouble. He was jailed. This made him mad. When released, he went to Algeria. He later returned to Morocco. He wanted to get even.

Hmara pretended to be the sultan's older brother. He claimed to be the rightful ruler. He set up his own government. He did this outside of the capital. He ruled from 1902 to 1909.

The new sultans were Abdelaziz (1881–1943) and Abd al-Hafid (1909–1912). They fought Hmara. They captured him. Hmara was put in a cage. He became part of the sultan's zoo. Some believe he was killed by lions. His remains were burned.

When returning to Morocco, Bou Hmara rode a female donkey. Bou Hmara means "the man on a female donkey."

ANNA ANDERSON

(1896–1984)

A **czar** is a Russian king. Czar Nicholas II (1868–1918) led the Romanov family. The Romanovs had ruled Russia for over 300 years. The czar and his family were killed in 1918. Their bodies weren't found until 1979. The bodies were examined in 1991. But two bodies were missing. One was the prince. Another was one of the princesses. People thought it was Anastasia.

A woman named Anna Anderson lived in Germany. In 1922, she claimed to be Anastasia. She said two men helped her escape from Russia. She later moved to New York City. She was treated like a star. Some people believed her. Some didn't.

In the 1980s, DNA testing was invented. DNA testing proved Anderson was lying. Anderson's real name was Franziska Schanzkowska. She was Polish. She was a factory worker. She had used the name Anna Anderson during a hotel visit. The name stuck.

The Romanov family was killed in 1918.

JOHN ROLAND REDD
(1921–1998)

* * * * * * * * * * *

John Roland Redd was born in Missouri. He was a Black musician. He wrote his own songs. He played the piano.

Redd faced racism. People didn't know much about India. So Redd created a new identity. He named himself Korla Pandit. He said he was from India. He said his mother was a French opera singer. He said his father was an Indian official. He said he studied music in England. He pretended to be Pandit all the time. He even wore a **turban**. A turban is a head covering.

Redd was a TV star. He had his own show. It was called *Korla Pandit's Adventures in Music*. It was the first all-music TV show. Redd never spoke on TV. He played the piano. He gazed into the camera. After he died, a magazine uncovered his secret.

John Roland Redd wore a traditional Sikh turban like the one below. Except he wore a jewel on the front. He claimed to be Hindu.

FOR YOUR EYES ONLY...

* * * * * * * * * *

HOW TO BE AN IMPOSTER!*

Do you want to be an imposter? Do you have what it takes? Here are 3 tips:

Tip #1: Have a good cover story.

A **cover story** hides the truth. It's your fake identity. Only include things you can recall. Don't mix up details. Say nothing that can be questioned. Keep it simple.

Tip #2: Don't attract attention.

Stay out of public notice. Stay off social media. Avoid pictures. Avoid fame. Don't let people identify you.

Tip #3: Distract haters.

People will question you. Turn their attention to something else. Talk about a hot topic. Pretend to drop something. Make excuses to leave. Don't defend yourself.

*WARNING: Imposters can go to jail. They can make people angry. They always have to hide. Don't be an imposter. Be yourself!

ICYW: IN CASE YOU'RE WONDERING...

The Science Behind Imposters

Imposters tell so many lies. Why do we believe these lies? We believe what we want to be true. This is wishful thinking. We're willing to ignore lies. We prefer fiction to fact. We want simple answers. We trust what people say. It's painful to know someone we trust is lying to us. Believing in lies protects us from being hurt. In some cases, we deny the truth. We may feel foolish. We may feel angry and ashamed. To avoid this, we keep believing the lies. Lies can comfort us. It's human nature to want familiar things. What's familiar becomes fact. We must work hard to break through lies. It's important to question things. It's important to find evidence.

GLOSSARY

confession (kuhn-FEH-shuhn) a formal acknowledgment or statement of truth

confidence (KAHN-fuh-duhns) belief in oneself, trust

cover story (KUH-vuhr STOR-ee) an invented story used to conceal the truth

czar (ZAHR) an emperor or king in Russia

deserted (dih-ZUHR-tuhd) left the military without permission

DNA testing (DNA TEH-sting) genetic tests that are used to detect changes or relationships

exploited (ik-SPLOY-tuhd) used for personal gain

imposters (im-PAH-stuhrz) a person who practices deception under an assumed character, identity, or name

intellectuals (in-tuh-LEK-chuh-wuhl) highly educated people

pardoned (PAR-duhnd) forgave

sacrificed (SAH-kruh-feyst) killed someone as an offering to a god

sultan (SUHL-tuhn) the ruler of some Islamic countries

treason (TREE-zuhn) the act of betraying one's government

turban (TUHR-buhn) a long, wrapped cloth worn as a headdress

LEARN MORE!

DuMont, Brianna. *Famous Phonies: Legends, Fakes, and Frauds Who Changed History*. New York, NY: Sky Pony, 2014.

DuMont, Brianna. *Thrilling Thieves: Liars, Cheats, and Cons Who Changed History*. New York, NY: Sky Pony, 2018.

Graham, Ian. *The Ultimate Book of Imposters: Over 100 True Stories of the Greatest Phonies and Frauds*. Naperville, IL: Sourcebooks, 2013.

INDEX